CYBER THREATS
DOXING

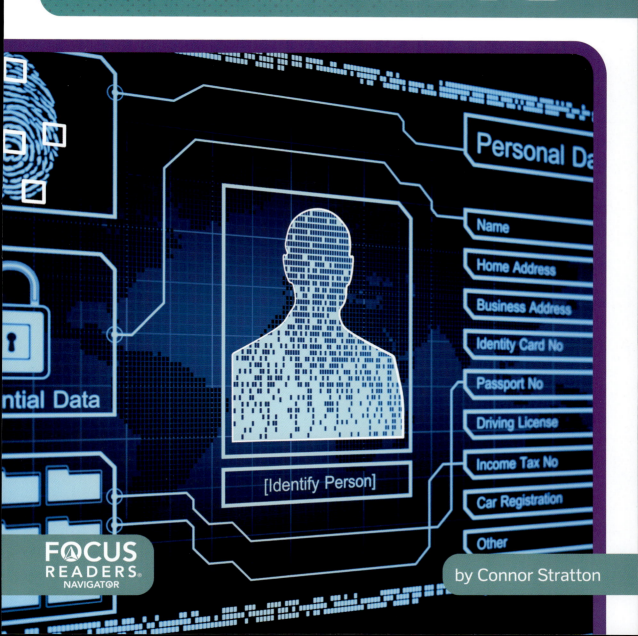

by Connor Stratton

WWW.FOCUSREADERS.COM

Copyright © 2026 by Focus Readers®, Mendota Heights, MN 55120. All rights reserved. No part of this book may be reproduced or utilized in any form or by any means without written permission from the publisher.

Focus Readers is distributed by North Star Editions:
sales@northstareditions.com | 888-417-0195

Produced for Focus Readers by Red Line Editorial.

Photographs ©: iStockphoto, cover, 1; Shutterstock Images, 4–5, 8–9, 13, 14–15, 17, 20–21, 23, 25, 26, 29; Rick Bowmer/AP Images, 7; Red Line Editorial, 11; Vernon Yuen/NurPhoto/AP Images, 19

Library of Congress Cataloging-in-Publication Data
Library of Congress Cataloging-in-Publication Data is available on the Library of Congress website.

ISBN
979-8-88998-518-1 (hardcover)
979-8-88998-579-2 (ebook pdf)
979-8-88998-550-1 (hosted ebook)

Printed in the United States of America
Mankato, MN
082025

ABOUT THE AUTHOR
Connor Stratton writes and edits nonfiction children's books. He lives in Minnesota.

TABLE OF CONTENTS

CHAPTER 1
Doxing the Doctors 5

CHAPTER 2
How It Works 9

CHAPTER 3
Purpose and Impact 15

CHAPTER 4
Fighting Doxing 21

CYBER SAFETY
Digital Footprints and Security 28

Focus Questions • 30
Glossary • 31
To Learn More • 32
Index • 32

CHAPTER 1

DOXING THE DOCTORS

In early 2020, a new disease spread quickly around the world. It was called COVID-19. The **pandemic** killed many people. Even more people became seriously ill.

COVID-19 was highly **contagious**. It spread through the air. For this reason, many governments required lockdowns.

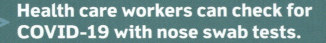
Health care workers can check for COVID-19 with nose swab tests.

That meant people could not gather indoors outside of their homes. Many areas required people to wear masks. These steps slowed the spread of COVID-19. They saved many lives.

Even so, people's daily lives changed. Some people felt they had lost their freedom. In addition, false information spread online. Several groups claimed the disease was fake. Others said the government planned to control people.

As a result, many health care workers faced **harassment**. Some people blamed workers for how their lives had changed. Some people even found out where local health care workers lived. Then they

Protesters stand outside the home of a Utah Department of Health worker in 2020.

shared their home addresses online. This act is called doxing.

Targeted workers often felt fear and stress. Some needed security teams to keep them safe. Others left their jobs. These events showed how harmful doxing could be.

CHAPTER 2

HOW IT WORKS

Doxing is the act of sharing someone's private information online. It happens without the victim's permission. When personal information becomes public, strangers may harass the victim.

Sometimes doxers make the victims' full names public. Other times, doxers release emails and phone numbers.

> The word *doxing* comes from the word *documents*. Doxers may share documents with personal information.

Doxing may include peoples' home addresses, places of work, and banking information. Personal photos, videos, or messages may be released, too.

A doxer uses many methods to find information. Simple internet searches

SMART GLASSES

Tech is always advancing. These changes often bring new opportunities. But they may also bring new threats. In 2024, two college students showed the threats of smart glasses. Smart glasses have **facial recognition**. The wearer can match someone's face to an online profile. Then, the wearer could easily share the other person's information. In this way, smart glasses could help someone dox others very quickly.

are common. For example, a doxer may use a social media account. They see the victim's username on that site. Then, the doxer searches the internet for that username. Accounts with the same name might appear on other sites.

GIVING INFORMATION TO DOXERS

Suppose you post an image of yourself at a café. Doxers can learn a lot of information from it.

Some doxers **cyberstalk** their victims. They look at images that people post online. Those images can reveal personal information. Some contain the users' locations.

Doxers may also use data brokers. These companies gather information about people online. For example, data brokers pay apps for users' data. Brokers often sell it to advertising companies. Individuals can buy the data, too.

Information from data brokers can be personal. For instance, many people use mapping apps. These apps can show where people live. They can also show people's daily routines.

Some doxers pretend to be police officers or security officials. Then they request personal information from tech companies.

Once doxers have personal information, they share it online. Suddenly, many strangers know the victim's details. They can harass that person. Strangers may send hateful messages. They may leave threatening voicemails. People may even spread lies to the victim's workplace, school, or neighbors.

CHAPTER 3

PURPOSE AND IMPACT

People dox others for several reasons. Personal reasons such as revenge and anger are common. Perhaps someone was broken up with. Or maybe the person lost a video game. This person may be angry. In response, the person might dox someone else. Then, **trolls** are able to harass the victim. Some trolls send

Sometimes content creators such as streamers get doxed by angry audience members.

hateful messages. Others post fake, embarrassing photos.

Money is another reason for doxing. Sometimes, people ask a victim for money. They threaten to dox the person unless they are paid. Other times,

GAMERGATE

For years, men dominated the video game business. That started to change in the 2010s. Women began gaining more recognition for their work. They also started speaking out against **sexism**. Some male gamers did not like these changes. They began harassing women who worked in video games. They doxed several women. These events became known as Gamergate.

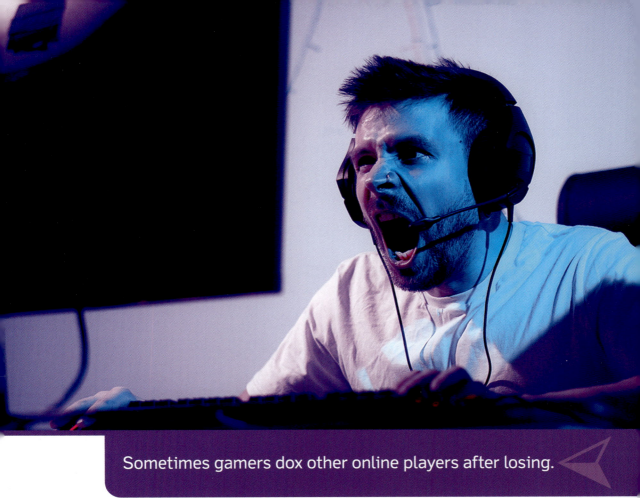

Sometimes gamers dox other online players after losing.

doxers share people's banking or credit card information. Strangers can use that information to buy things.

Sometimes people dox as a form of **activism**. For example, some doxers may disagree with a hate group. So, they expose members of the group. Doxing is a way to shame those people in public.

Journalists often face threats of doxing. Reporters may write about the harmful behavior of others. Doxing can be a way to silence those reporters.

Doxing can be harmful to victims. Online harassment causes fear, stress, and shame. People may lose money. They can lose their jobs. Sometimes doxing even results in violence. Swatting is one example. That's when someone calls the police on a doxing victim. The caller says the person is being violent. So, the police go to the doxing victim's house. They bring a SWAT team. The experience is

In 2024, a Hong Kong reporter spoke about journalists being doxed for political reasons.

terrifying for the victim. In some cases, people have been killed during swatting.

Doxing can have wider effects, too. People may become less willing to share their opinions. They don't want to risk being doxed if others disagree with them. Over time, people may become less trusting of others.

CHAPTER 4

FIGHTING DOXING

People can fight against doxing in several ways. Laws against doxing can help. By 2025, a few countries had made doxing a crime. Several US states had also passed laws against it. Some laws let victims sue the doxers. However, most experts believed it wasn't enough. They said more governments had to take

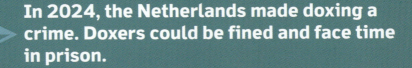

In 2024, the Netherlands made doxing a crime. Doxers could be fined and face time in prison.

stronger action. In most places, doxing victims still had to rely on laws against hacking or stalking. Existing laws did not do enough about doxing in particular.

Governments have responded in other ways, too. In 2018, for example, Seattle police took a new approach to swatting.

DOXING IN HONG KONG

In 2019, large protests began in Hong Kong. Police often responded brutally. Protesters tried to counter police in a variety of ways. Some doxed police officers. Supporters of the government began doxing protesters, too. In 2021, Hong Kong made doxing a crime. Some security experts supported the new law. Others worried it would help the government silence any protesters.

Having more information can help SWAT teams be less likely to use force on innocent people.

They asked people to alert the police if they were worried about being swatted. Police kept that information. Then, if someone called the police about the person, the police would know that the call might be a swatting attempt.

Tech companies also play a role. These companies control platforms where people enter personal information. Some companies make it easy to find this data. But experts say they should do more to protect the data. Facebook made this type of change in 2022. The company stopped letting users share home addresses.

Tech companies can also create more ways to block doxing. They can work on noticing and stopping it. For example, companies can hire **moderators**. These workers look for harmful behavior on sites. Users can also report doxing to moderators. Then moderators can quickly

Moderators carefully check anything that looks unusual or harmful.

delete posts or ban users. Companies can also use computer programs to help. Some programs can spot doxing **automatically**. Then the companies can take action.

25

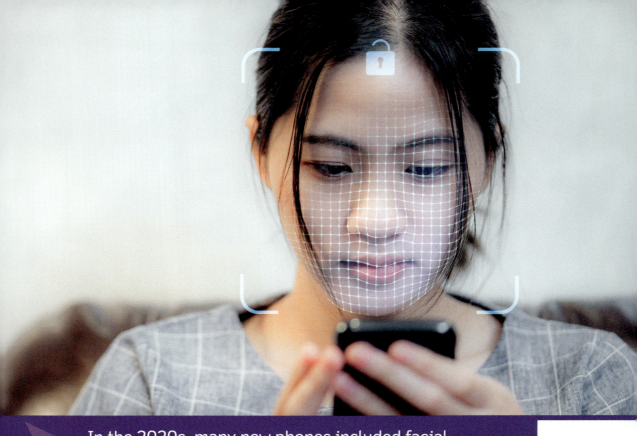

In the 2020s, many new phones included facial recognition software for security.

Improving cybersecurity can also help. For instance, some tools can help prevent hacking. One method is called two-factor authentication. This method requires two steps to log in to an account. The first step is a password. The second step can be a few different things. It may be a question only the user can answer. It could be a fingerprint or facial scan. Or it may send a notice to another device. With two-factor authentication, hackers have a harder time gaining access to personal information. That makes it more difficult for hackers to dox people.

    Individuals can also take steps to fight doxing. For example, they can shrink their digital footprints. A digital footprint is all the ways that someone's identity is available online. If someone's footprint is smaller, other people can't find as much about them online. Their personal information is safer from doxing.

> CYBER SAFETY

DIGITAL FOOTPRINTS AND SECURITY

Individuals can take many steps to make their digital footprints smaller. First, a person needs to know what their footprint is. They should search their name online. For example, a person can use an image of themselves. Then, they can do an image search with it. Next, they can examine the results. The search shows what websites have that photo. After that, people can delete it.

People can use safer practices online, too. People should avoid sharing personal information on social media. For example, it is safer to avoid sharing full names. People should never post their address. Not posting photos of themselves or family members helps, too.

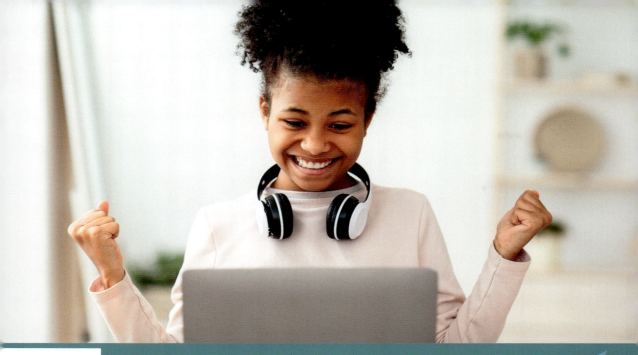

Small, simple actions can help keep people safe from doxing.

In addition, people should secure their accounts. That includes using strong passwords. Strong passwords are long. They use letters, numbers, and symbols. Also, each account should have a different password. Then, a hacker may get into one account. But they can't get into others. People can also use two-factor authentication.

Privacy settings can help, too. On each site, users should choose the most private option. That limits the data the site gathers and shares. These actions help protect against doxing.

FOCUS QUESTIONS

Write your answers on a separate piece of paper.

1. Write a paragraph explaining the main ideas of Chapter 3.

2. Do you think you need to decrease your digital footprint? Why or why not?

3. What is one feature of a strong password?
    - **A.** The password is the same on every account.
    - **B.** The password is very short and simple.
    - **C.** The password is long and complicated.

4. What is one way people can avoid being doxed?
    - **A.** They can avoid sharing personal details online.
    - **B.** They can share images of themselves online.
    - **C.** They can use weaker privacy settings.

Answer key on page 32.

GLOSSARY

activism
Actions to make social or political changes.

automatically
Done on its own, without any outside control.

contagious
Able to spread to other people.

cyberstalk
To follow others online in a threatening, unwanted way.

facial recognition
Using images of people's faces to figure out who they are.

harassment
Behavior that makes someone feel unsafe or uncomfortable.

moderators
People who run online sites or groups and make sure users follow the rules.

pandemic
A disease that spreads quickly around the world.

sexism
Hatred or mistreatment of people because of their gender.

trolls
People who post messages that are meant to upset others.

TO LEARN MORE

BOOKS

Carser, A. R. *Protect Your Data and Identity Online*. BrightPoint Press, 2022.

Clark, Katie. *Dealing with Online Bullies*. Lerner Publications, 2026.

Spanier, Kristine, MLIS. *Digital Footprint*. Jump!, 2025.

NOTE TO EDUCATORS

Visit **www.focusreaders.com** to find lesson plans, activities, links, and other resources related to this title.

INDEX

activism, 17

COVID-19, 5–6
cybersecurity, 26
cyberstalking, 12

data brokers, 12
digital footprints, 27, 28

Facebook, 24
facial recognition, 10

hacking, 22, 26–27, 29
harassment, 6, 9, 13, 15–16, 18
Hong Kong, 22

journalists, 18

moderators, 24

pandemic, 5
police, 18, 22–23
privacy, 9, 29

social media, 11, 28
swatting, 18–19, 22–23

tech companies, 24–25
trolls, 15–16
two-factor authentication, 26–27, 29

video games, 15–16

Answer Key: 1. Answers will vary; 2. Answers will vary; 3. C; 4. A